Pocket Edition

Lord Byron

THE ISLAND

Christian and his Comrades

The Island, or

Christian and his Comrades

George Gordon Byron

ISBN: 978-0-9953520-7-0

This pocket edition made available by Jonathon Best

For more poetry and classic pocket editions, check out

jbestbooks.com

&

amazon.com/author/jonbest

CANTO THE FIRST

The morning watch was come; the vessel lay
  Her course, and gently made her liquid way;
The cloven billow flashed from off her prow
In furrows formed by that majestic plough;
The waters with their world were all before;
Behind, the South Sea's many an islet shore.
The quiet night, now dappling, 'gan to wane,
Dividing darkness from the dawning main;
The dolphins, not unconscious of the day,
Swam high, as eager of the coming ray;
The stars from broader beams began to creep,
And lift their shining eyelids from the deep;
The sail resumed its lately shadowed white,
And the wind fluttered with a freshening flight;
The purpling Ocean owns the coming Sun,
But ere he break—a deed is to be done.
The gallant Chief within his cabin slept,
Secure in those by whom the watch was kept:
His dreams were of Old England's welcome shore,
Of toils rewarded, and of dangers o'er;

His name was added to the glorious roll

Of those who search the storm-surrounded Pole.

The worst was over, and the rest seemed sure,

And why should not his slumber be secure?

Alas! his deck was trod by unwilling feet,

And wilder hands would hold the vessel's sheet;

Young hearts, which languished for some sunny isle,

Where summer years and summer women smile;

Men without country, who, too long estranged,

Had found no native home, or found it changed,

And, half uncivilised, preferred the cave

Of some soft savage to the uncertain wave—

The gushing fruits that nature gave unfilled;

The wood without a path—but where they willed;

The field o'er which promiscuous Plenty poured

Her horn; the equal land without a lord;

The wish—which ages have not yet subdued

In man—to have no master save his mood;

The earth, whose mine was on its face, unsold,

The glowing sun and produce all its gold;

The Freedom which can call each grot a home;

The general garden, where all steps may roam,

Where Nature owns a nation as her child,

Exulting in the enjoyment of the wild;

Their shells, their fruits, the only wealth they know,

Their unexploring navy, the canoe;

Their sport, the dashing breakers and the chase;

Their strangest sight, an European face:—

Such was the country which these strangers yearned

To see again—a sight they dearly earned.

Awake, bold Bligh! the foe is at the gate!

Awake! awake!——Alas! it is too late!

Fiercely beside thy cot the mutineer

Stands, and proclaims the reign of rage and fear.

Thy limbs are bound, the bayonet at thy breast;

The hands, which trembled at thy voice, arrest;

Dragged o'er the deck, no more at thy command

The obedient helm shall veer, the sail expand;

That savage Spirit, which would lull by wrath

Its desperate escape from Duty's path,

Glares round thee, in the scarce believing eyes

Of those who fear the Chief they sacrifice:

For ne'er can Man his conscience all assuage,

Unless he drain the wine of Passion—Rage.

In vain, not silenced by the eye of Death,

Thou call'st the loyal with thy menaced breath:—

They come not; they are few, and, overawed,

Must acquiesce, while sterner hearts applaud.

In vain thou dost demand the cause: a curse

Is all the answer, with the threat of worse.

Full in thine eyes is waved the glittering blade,

Close to thy throat the pointed bayonet laid.

The levelled muskets circle round thy breast

In hands as steeled to do the deadly rest.

Thou dar'st them to their worst, exclaiming—"Fire!"

But they who pitied not could yet admire;

Some lurking remnant of their former awe

Restrained them longer than their broken law;

They would not dip their souls at once in blood,

But left thee to the mercies of the flood.

"Hoist out the boat!" was now the leader's cry;

And who dare answer "No!" to Mutiny,

In the first dawning of the drunken hour,

The Saturnalia of unhoped-for power?

The boat is lowered with all the haste of hate,

With its slight plank between thee and thy fate;

Her only cargo such a scant supply

As promises the death their hands deny;

And just enough of water and of bread

To keep, some days, the dying from the dead:

Some cordage, canvass, sails, and lines, and twine,

But treasures all to hermits of the brine,

Were added after, to the earnest prayer

Of those who saw no hope, save sea and air;

And last, that trembling vassal of the Pole—

The feeling compass—Navigation's soul.

And now the self-elected Chief finds time

To stun the first sensation of his crime,

And raise it in his followers—"Ho! the bowl!"

Lest passion should return to reason's shoal.

"Brandy for heroes!" Burke could once exclaim—
No doubt a liquid path to Epic fame;
And such the new-born heroes found it here,
And drained the draught with an applauding cheer.
"Huzza! for Otaheite!" was the cry.
How strange such shouts from sons of Mutiny!
The gentle island, and the genial soil,
The friendly hearts, the feasts without a toil,
The courteous manners but from nature caught,
The wealth unhoarded, and the love unbought;
Could these have charms for rudest sea-boys, driven
Before the mast by every wind of heaven?
And now, even now prepared with others' woes
To earn mild Virtue's vain desire, repose?
Alas! such is our nature! all but aim
At the same end by pathways not the same;
Our means—our birth—our nation, and our name,
Our fortune—temper—even our outward frame,
Are far more potent o'er our yielding clay
Than aught we know beyond our little day.

Yet still there whispers the small voice within,

Heard through Gain's silence, and o'er Glory's din:

Whatever creed be taught, or land be trod,

Man's conscience is the Oracle of God.

The launch is crowded with the faithful few

Who wait their Chief, a melancholy crew:

But some remained reluctant on the deck

Of that proud vessel—now a moral wreck—

And viewed their Captain's fate with piteous eyes;

While others scoffed his augured miseries,

Sneered at the prospect of his pigmy sail,

And the slight bark so laden and so frail.

The tender nautilus, who steers his prow,

The sea-born sailor of his shell canoe,

The ocean Mab, the fairy of the sea,

Seems far less fragile, and, alas! more free.

He, when the lightning-winged Tornados sweep

The surge, is safe—his port is in the deep—

And triumphs o'er the armadas of Mankind,

Which shake the World, yet crumble in the wind.

When all was now prepared, the vessel clear
Which hailed her master in the mutineer,
A seaman, less obdurate than his mates,
Showed the vain pity which but irritates;
Watched his late Chieftain with exploring eye,
And told, in signs, repentant sympathy;
Held the moist shaddock to his parched mouth,
Which felt Exhaustion's deep and bitter drouth.
But soon observed, this guardian was withdrawn,
Nor further Mercy clouds Rebellion's dawn.
Then forward stepped the bold and froward boy
His Chief had cherished only to destroy,
And, pointing to the helpless prow beneath,
Exclaimed, "Depart at once! delay is death!"
Yet then, even then, his feelings ceased not all:
In that last moment could a word recall
Remorse for the black deed as yet half done,
And what he hid from many showed to one:
When Bligh in stern reproach demanded where
Was now his grateful sense of former care?

Where all his hopes to see his name aspire,

And blazon Britain's thousand glories higher?

His feverish lips thus broke their gloomy spell,

"Tis that! 'tis that! I am in hell! in hell!"

No more he said; but urging to the bark

His Chief, commits him to his fragile ark;

These the sole accents from his tongue that fell,

But volumes lurked below his fierce farewell.

The arctic Sun rose broad above the wave;

The breeze now sank, now whispered from his cave;

As on the Æolian harp, his fitful wings

Now swelled, now fluttered o'er his Ocean strings.

With slow, despairing oar, the abandoned skiff

Ploughs its drear progress to the scarce seen cliff,

Which lifts its peak a cloud above the main:

That boat and ship shall never meet again!

But 'tis not mine to tell their tale of grief,

Their constant peril, and their scant relief;

Their days of danger, and their nights of pain;

Their manly courage even when deemed in vain;

The sapping famine, rendering scarce a son
Known to his mother in the skeleton;
The ills that lessened still their little store,
And starved even Hunger till he wrung no more;
The varying frowns and favours of the deep,
That now almost ingulfs, then leaves to creep
With crazy oar and shattered strength along
The tide that yields reluctant to the strong;
The incessant fever of that arid thirst
Which welcomes, as a well, the clouds that burst
Above their naked bones, and feels delight
In the cold drenching of the stormy night,
And from the outspread canvass gladly wrings
A drop to moisten Life's all-gasping springs;
The savage foe escaped, to seek again
More hospitable shelter from the main;
The ghastly Spectres which were doomed at last
To tell as true a tale of dangers past,
As ever the dark annals of the deep
Disclosed for man to dread or woman weep.

We leave them to their fate, but not unknown

Nor unredressed. Revenge may have her own:

Roused Discipline aloud proclaims their cause,

And injured Navies urge their broken laws.

Pursue we on his track the mutineer,

Whom distant vengeance had not taught to fear.

Wide o'er the wave—away! away! away!

Once more his eyes shall hail the welcome bay;

Once more the happy shores without a law

Receive the outlaws whom they lately saw;

Nature, and Nature's goddess—Woman—woos

To lands where, save their conscience, none accuse;

Where all partake the earth without dispute,

And bread itself is gathered as a fruit;

Where none contest the fields, the woods, the streams:—

The goldless Age, where Gold disturbs no dreams,

Inhabits or inhabited the shore,

Till Europe taught them better than before;

Bestowed her customs, and amended theirs,

But left her vices also to their heirs.

Away with this! behold them as they were,

Do good with Nature, or with Nature err.

"Huzza! for Otaheite!" was the cry,

As stately swept the gallant vessel by.

The breeze springs up; the lately flapping sail

Extends its arch before the growing gale;

In swifter ripples stream aside the seas,

Which her bold bow flings off with dashing ease.

Thus Argo ploughed the Euxine's virgin foam,

But those she wafted still looked back to home;

These spurn their country with their rebel bark,

And fly her as the raven fled the Ark;

And yet they seek to nestle with the dove,

And tame their fiery spirits down to Love.

CANTO THE SECOND

How pleasant were the songs of Toobonai,
When Summer's Sun went down the coral bay!
Come, let us to the islet's softest shade,
And hear the warbling birds! the damsels said:
The wood-dove from the forest depth shall coo,
Like voices of the Gods from Bolotoo;
We'll cull the flowers that grow above the dead,
For these most bloom where rests the warrior's head;
And we will sit in Twilight's face, and see
The sweet Moon glancing through the Tooa tree,
The lofty accents of whose sighing bough
Shall sadly please us as we lean below;
Or climb the steep, and view the surf in vain
Wrestle with rocky giants o'er the main,
Which spurn in columns back the baffled spray.
How beautiful are these! how happy they,
Who, from the toil and tumult of their lives,
Steal to look down where nought but Ocean strives!
Even He too loves at times the blue lagoon,
And smooths his ruffled mane beneath the Moon.

Yes—from the sepulchre we'll gather flowers,

Then feast like spirits in their promised bowers,

Then plunge and revel in the rolling surf,

Then lay our limbs along the tender turf,

And, wet and shining from the sportive toil,

Anoint our bodies with the fragrant oil,

And plait our garlands gathered from the grave,

And wear the wreaths that sprung from out the brave.

But lo! night comes, the Mooa woos us back,

The sound of mats are heard along our track;

Anon the torchlight dance shall fling its sheen

In flashing mazes o'er the Marly's green;

And we too will be there; we too recall

The memory bright with many a festival,

Ere Fiji blew the shell of war, when foes

For the first time were wafted in canoes.

Alas! for them the flower of manhood bleeds;

Alas! for them our fields are rank with weeds:

Forgotten is the rapture, or unknown,

Of wandering with the Moon and Love alone.

But be it so:—they taught us how to wield

The club, and rain our arrows o'er the field:

Now let them reap the harvest of their art!

But feast to-night! to-morrow we depart.

Strike up the dance! the Cava bowl fill high!

Drain every drop!—to-morrow we may die.

In summer garments be our limbs arrayed;

Around our waists the Tappa's white displayed;

Thick wreaths shall form our coronal, like Spring's,

And round our necks shall glance the Hooni strings;

So shall their brighter hues contrast the glow

Of the dusk bosoms that beat high below.

But now the dance is o'er—yet stay awhile;

Ah, pause! nor yet put out the social smile.

To-morrow for the Mooa we depart,

But not to-night—to-night is for the heart.

Again bestow the wreaths we gently woo,

Ye young Enchantresses of gay Licoo!

How lovely are your forms! how every sense

Bows to your beauties, softened, but intense,

Like to the flowers on Mataloco's steep,

Which fling their fragrance far athwart the deep!—

We too will see Licoo; but—oh! my heart!—

What do I say?—to-morrow we depart!

Thus rose a song—the harmony of times

Before the winds blew Europe o'er these climes.

True, they had vices—such are Nature's growth—

But only the barbarian's—we have both;

The sordor of civilisation, mixed

With all the savage which Man's fall hath fixed.

Who hath not seen Dissimulation's reign,

The prayers of Abel linked to deeds of Cain?

Who such would see may from his lattice view

The Old World more degraded than the New,—

Now new no more, save where Columbia rears

Twin giants, born by Freedom to her spheres,

Where Chimborazo, over air,—earth,—wave,—

Glares with his Titan eye, and sees no slave.

Such was this ditty of Tradition's days,

Which to the dead a lingering fame conveys

In song, where Fame as yet hath left no sign
Beyond the sound whose charm is half divine;
Which leaves no record to the sceptic eye,
But yields young History all to Harmony;
A boy Achilles, with the Centaur's lyre
In hand, to teach him to surpass his sire.
For one long-cherished ballad's simple stave,
Rung from the rock, or mingled with the wave,
Or from the bubbling streamlet's grassy side,
Or gathering mountain echoes as they glide,
Hath greater power o'er each true heart and ear,
Than all the columns Conquest's minions rear;
Invites, when Hieroglyphics are a theme
For sages' labours, or the student's dream;
Attracts, when History's volumes are a toil,—
The first, the freshest bud of Feeling's soil.
Such was this rude rhyme—rhyme is of the rude—
But such inspired the Norseman's solitude,
Who came and conquered; such, wherever rise
Lands which no foes destroy or civilise,

Exist: and what can our accomplished art

Of verse do more than reach the awakened heart?

And sweetly now those untaught melodies

Broke the luxurious silence of the skies,

The sweet siesta of a summer day,

The tropic afternoon of Toobonai,

When every flower was bloom, and air was balm,

And the first breath began to stir the palm,

The first yet voiceless wind to urge the wave

All gently to refresh the thirsty cave,

Where sat the Songstress with the stranger boy,

Who taught her Passion's desolating joy,

Too powerful over every heart, but most

O'er those who know not how it may be lost;

O'er those who, burning in the new-born fire,

Like martyrs revel in their funeral pyre,

With such devotion to their ecstacy,

That Life knows no such rapture as to die:

And die they do; for earthly life has nought

Matched with that burst of Nature, even in thought;

And all our dreams of better life above
But close in one eternal gush of Love.
There sat the gentle savage of the wild,
In growth a woman, though in years a child,
As childhood dates within our colder clime,
Where nought is ripened rapidly save crime;
The infant of an infant world, as pure
From Nature—lovely, warm, and premature;
Dusky like night, but night with all her stars;
Or cavern sparkling with its native spars;
With eyes that were a language and a spell,
A form like Aphrodite's in her shell,
With all her loves around her on the deep,
Voluptuous as the first approach of sleep;
Yet full of life—for through her tropic cheek
The blush would make its way, and all but speak;
The sun-born blood suffused her neck, and threw
O'er her clear nut-brown skin a lucid hue,
Like coral reddening through the darkened wave,
Which draws the diver to the crimson cave.

Such was this daughter of the southern seas,

Herself a billow in her energies,

To bear the bark of others' happiness,

Nor feel a sorrow till their joy grew less:

Her wild and warm yet faithful bosom knew

No joy like what it gave; her hopes ne'er drew

Aught from Experience, that chill touchstone, whose

Sad proof reduces all things from their hues:

She feared no ill, because she knew it not,

Or what she knew was soon—too soon—forgot:

Her smiles and tears had passed, as light winds pass

O'er lakes to ruffle, not destroy, their glass,

Whose depths unsearched, and fountains from the hill,

Restore their surface, in itself so still,

Until the Earthquake tear the Naiad's cave,

Root up the spring, and trample on the wave,

And crush the living waters to a mass,

The amphibious desert of the dank morass!

And must their fate be hers? The eternal change

But grasps Humanity with quicker range;

And they who fall but fall as worlds will fall,

To rise, if just, a Spirit o'er them all.

And who is he? the blue-eyed northern child

Of isles more known to man, but scarce less wild;

The fair-haired offspring of the Hebrides,

Where roars the Pentland with its whirling seas;

Rocked in his cradle by the roaring wind,

The tempest-born in body and in mind,

His young eyes opening on the ocean-foam,

Had from that moment deemed the deep his home,

The giant comrade of his pensive moods,

The sharer of his craggy solitudes,

The only Mentor of his youth, where'er

His bark was borne; the sport of wave and air;

A careless thing, who placed his choice in chance,

Nursed by the legends of his land's romance;

Eager to hope, but not less firm to bear,

Acquainted with all feelings save despair.

Placed in the Arab's clime he would have been

As bold a rover as the sands have seen,

And braved their thirst with as enduring lip
As Ishmael, wafted on his Desert-Ship;
Fixed upon Chili's shore, a proud cacique:
On Hellas' mountains, a rebellious Greek;
Born in a tent, perhaps a Tamerlane;
Bred to a throne, perhaps unfit to reign.
For the same soul that rends its path to sway,
If reared to such, can find no further prey
Beyond itself, and must retrace its way,
Plunging for pleasure into pain: the same
Spirit which made a Nero, Rome's worst shame,
A humbler state and discipline of heart,
Had formed his glorious namesake's counterpart;
But grant his vices, grant them all his own,
How small their theatre without a throne!
Thou smilest:—these comparisons seem high
To those who scan all things with dazzled eye;
Linked with the unknown name of one whose doom
Has nought to do with glory or with Rome,
With Chili, Hellas, or with Araby;—
Thou smilest?—Smile; 'tis better thus than sigh;

Yet such he might have been; he was a man,

A soaring spirit, ever in the van,

A patriot hero or despotic chief,

To form a nation's glory or its grief,

Born under auspices which make us more

Or less than we delight to ponder o'er.

But these are visions; say, what was he here?

A blooming boy, a truant mutineer.

The fair-haired Torquil, free as Ocean's spray,

The husband of the bride of Toobonai.

By Neuha's side he sate, and watched the waters,—

Neuha, the sun-flower of the island daughters,

Highborn, (a birth at which the herald smiles,

Without a scutcheon for these secret isles,)

Of a long race, the valiant and the free,

The naked knights of savage chivalry,

Whose grassy cairns ascend along the shore;

And thine—I've seen—Achilles! do no more.

She, when the thunder-bearing strangers came,

In vast canoes, begirt with bolts of flame,

Topped with tall trees, which, loftier than the palm,

Seemed rooted in the deep amidst its calm:

But when the winds awakened, shot forth wings

Broad as the cloud along the horizon flings,

And swayed the waves, like cities of the sea,

Making the very billows look less free;—

She, with her paddling oar and dancing prow,

Shot through the surf, like reindeer through the snow,

Swift-gliding o'er the breaker's whitening edge,

Light as a Nereid in her ocean sledge,

And gazed and wondered at the giant hulk,

Which heaved from wave to wave its trampling bulk.

The anchor dropped; it lay along the deep,

Like a huge lion in the sun asleep,

While round it swarmed the Proas' flitting chain,

Like summer bees that hum around his mane.

The white man landed!—need the rest be told?

The New World stretched its dusk hand to the Old;

Each was to each a marvel, and the tie

Of wonder warmed to better sympathy.

Kind was the welcome of the sun-born sires,

And kinder still their daughters' gentler fires.

Their union grew: the children of the storm

Found beauty linked with many a dusky form;

While these in turn admired the paler glow,

Which seemed so white in climes that knew no snow.

The chace, the race, the liberty to roam,

The soil where every cottage showed a home;

The sea-spread net, the lightly launched canoe,

Which stemmed the studded archipelago,

O'er whose blue bosom rose the starry isles;

The healthy slumber, earned by sportive toils;

The palm, the loftiest Dryad of the woods,

Within whose bosom infant Bacchus broods,

While eagles scarce build higher than the crest

Which shadows o'er the vineyard in her breast;

The Cava feast, the Yam, the Cocoa's root,

Which bears at once the cup, and milk, and fruit;

The Bread-tree, which, without the ploughshare, yields

The unreaped harvest of unfurrowed fields,

And bakes its unadulterated loaves
Without a furnace in unpurchased groves,
And flings off famine from its fertile breast,
A priceless market for the gathering guest;—
These, with the luxuries of seas and woods,
The airy joys of social solitudes,
Tamed each rude wanderer to the sympathies
Of those who were more happy, if less wise,
Did more than Europe's discipline had done,
And civilised Civilisation's son!
Of these, and there was many a willing pair,
Neuha and Torquil were not the least fair:
Both children of the isles, though distant far;
Both born beneath a sea-presiding star;
Both nourished amidst Nature's native scenes,
Loved to the last, whatever intervenes
Between us and our Childhood's sympathy,
Which still reverts to what first caught the eye.
He who first met the Highlands' swelling blue
Will love each peak that shows a kindred hue,

Hail in each crag a friend's familiar face,

And clasp the mountain in his Mind's embrace.

Long have I roamed through lands which are not mine,

Adored the Alp, and loved the Apennine,

Revered Parnassus, and beheld the steep

Jove's Ida and Olympus crown the deep:

But 'twas not all long ages' lore, nor all

Their nature held me in their thrilling thrall;

The infant rapture still survived the boy,

And Loch-na-gar with Ida looked o'er Troy,

Mixed Celtic memories with the Phrygian mount,

And Highland linns with Castalie's clear fount.

Forgive me, Homer's universal shade!

Forgive me, Phœbus! that my fancy strayed;

The North and Nature taught me to adore

Your scenes sublime, from those beloved before.

The love which maketh all things fond and fair,

The youth which makes one rainbow of the air,

The dangers past, that make even Man enjoy

The pause in which he ceases to destroy,

The mutual beauty, which the sternest feel

Strike to their hearts like lightning to the steel,

United the half savage and the whole,

The maid and boy, in one absorbing soul.

No more the thundering memory of the fight

Wrapped his weaned bosom in its dark delight;

No more the irksome restlessness of Rest

Disturbed him like the eagle in her nest,

Whose whetted beak and far-pervading eye

Darts for a victim over all the sky:

His heart was tamed to that voluptuous state,

At once Elysian and effeminate,

Which leaves no laurels o'er the Hero's urn;—

These wither when for aught save blood they burn;

Yet when their ashes in their nook are laid,

Doth not the myrtle leave as sweet a shade?

Had Cæsar known but Cleopatra's kiss,

Rome had been free, the world had not been his.

And what have Cæsar's deeds and Cæsar's fame

Done for the earth? We feel them in our shame.

The gory sanction of his Glory stains

The rust which tyrants cherish on our chains.

Though Glory—Nature— Reason—Freedom, bid

Roused millions do what single Brutus did—

Sweep these mere mock-birds of the Despot's song

From the tall bough where they have perched so long,—

Still are we hawked at by such mousing owls,

And take for falcons those ignoble fowls,

When but a word of freedom would dispel

These bugbears, as their terrors show too well.

Rapt in the fond forgetfulness of life,

Neuha, the South Sea girl, was all a wife,

With no distracting world to call her off

From Love; with no Society to scoff

At the new transient flame; no babbling crowd

Of coxcombry in admiration loud,

Or with adulterous whisper to alloy

Her duty, and her glory, and her joy:

With faith and feelings naked as her form,

She stood as stands a rainbow in a storm,

Changing its hues with bright variety,

But still expanding lovelier o'er the sky,

Howe'er its arch may swell, its colours move,

The cloud-compelling harbinger of Love.

Here, in this grotto of the wave-worn shore,

They passed the Tropic's red meridian o'er;

Nor long the hours—they never paused o'er time,

Unbroken by the clock's funereal chime,

Which deals the daily pittance of our span,

And points and mocks with iron laugh at man.

What deemed they of the future or the past?

The present, like a tyrant, held them fast:

Their hour-glass was the sea-sand, and the tide,

Like her smooth billow, saw their moments glide

Their clock the Sun, in his unbounded tower

They reckoned not, whose day was but an hour;

The nightingale, their only vesper-bell,

Sung sweetly to the rose the day's farewell;

The broad Sun set, but not with lingering sweep,

As in the North he mellows o'er the deep;

But fiery, full, and fierce, as if he left
The World for ever, earth of light bereft,
Plunged with red forehead down along the wave,
As dives a hero headlong to his grave.
Then rose they, looking first along the skies,
And then for light into each other's eyes,
Wondering that Summer showed so brief a sun,
And asking if indeed the day were done.
And let not this seem strange: the devotee
Lives not in earth, but in his ecstasy;
Around him days and worlds are heedless driven,
His Soul is gone before his dust to Heaven.
Is Love less potent? No—his path is trod,
Alike uplifted gloriously to God;
Or linked to all we know of Heaven below,
The other better self, whose joy or woe
Is more than ours; the all-absorbing flame
Which, kindled by another, grows the same,
Wrapt in one blaze; the pure, yet funeral pile,
Where gentle hearts, like Bramins, sit and smile.

How often we forget all time, when lone,

Admiring Nature's universal throne,

Her woods—her wilds—her waters—the intense

Reply of hers to our intelligence!

Live not the Stars and Mountains? Are the Waves

Without a spirit? Are the dropping caves

Without a feeling in their silent tears?

No, no;—they woo and clasp us to their spheres,

Dissolve this clog and clod of clay before

Its hour, and merge our soul in the great shore.

Strip off this fond and false identity!—

Who thinks of self when gazing on the sky?

And who, though gazing lower, ever thought,

In the young moments ere the heart is taught

Time's lesson, of Man's baseness or his own?

All Nature is his realm, and Love his throne.

Neuha arose, and Torquil: Twilight's hour

Came sad and softly to their rocky bower,

Which, kindling by degrees its dewy spars,

Echoed their dim light to the mustering stars.

Slowly the pair, partaking Nature's calm,
Sought out their cottage, built beneath the palm;
Now smiling and now silent, as the scene;
Lovely as Love—the Spirit!—when serene.
The Ocean scarce spoke louder with his swell,
Than breathes his mimic murmurer in the shell,
As, far divided from his parent deep,
The sea-born infant cries, and will not sleep,
Raising his little plaint in vain, to rave
For the broad bosom of his nursing wave:
The woods drooped darkly, as inclined to rest,
The tropic bird wheeled rockward to his nest,
And the blue sky spread round them like a lake
Of peace, where Piety her thirst might slake.
But through the palm and plantain, hark, a Voice!
Not such as would have been a lover's choice,
In such an hour, to break the air so still;
No dying night-breeze, harping o'er the hill,
Striking the strings of nature, rock and tree,
Those best and earliest lyres of Harmony,

With Echo for their chorus; nor the alarm

Of the loud war-whoop to dispel the charm;

Nor the soliloquy of the hermit owl,

Exhaling all his solitary soul,

The dim though large-eyed wingéd anchorite,

Who peals his dreary Pæan o'er the night;

But a loud, long, and naval whistle, shrill

As ever started through a sea-bird's bill;

And then a pause, and then a hoarse "Hillo!

Torquil, my boy! what cheer? Ho! brother, ho!"

"Who hails?" cried Torquil, following with his eye

The sound. "Here's one," was all the brief reply.

But here the herald of the self-same mouth

Came breathing o'er the aromatic south,

Not like a "bed of violets" on the gale,

But such as wafts its cloud o'er grog or ale,

Borne from a short frail pipe, which yet had blown

Its gentle odours over either zone,

And, puffed where'er winds rise or waters roll,

Had wafted smoke from Portsmouth to the Pole,

Opposed its vapour as the lightning flashed,

And reeked, 'midst mountain-billows, unabashed,

To Æolus a constant sacrifice,

Through every change of all the varying skies.

And what was he who bore it?—I may err,

But deem him sailor or philosopher.

Sublime Tobacco! which from East to West

Cheers the tar's labour or the Turkman's rest;

Which on the Moslem's ottoman divides

His hours, and rivals opium and his brides;

Magnificent in Stamboul, but less grand,

Though not less loved, in Wapping or the Strand;

Divine in hookas, glorious in a pipe,

When tipped with amber, mellow, rich, and ripe:

Like other charmers, wooing the caress,

More dazzlingly when daring in full dress;

Yet thy true lovers more admire by far

Thy naked beauties—Give me a cigar!

Through the approaching darkness of the wood

A human figure broke the solitude,

Fantastically, it may be, arrayed,
A seaman in a savage masquerade;
Such as appears to rise out from the deep,
When o'er the line the merry vessels sweep,
And the rough Saturnalia of the tar
Flock o'er the deck, in Neptune's borrowed car;
And, pleased, the God of Ocean sees his name
Revive once more, though but in mimic game
Of his true sons, who riot in the breeze
Undreamt of in his native Cyclades.
Still the old God delights, from out the main,
To snatch some glimpses of his ancient reign.
Our sailor's jacket, though in ragged trim,
His constant pipe, which never yet burned dim,
His foremast air, and somewhat rolling gait,
Like his dear vessel, spoke his former state;
But then a sort of kerchief round his head,
Not over tightly bound, nor nicely spread;
And, 'stead of trowsers (ah! too early torn!
For even the mildest woods will have their thorn)

A curious sort of somewhat scanty mat
Now served for inexpressibles and hat;
His naked feet and neck, and sunburnt face,
Perchance might suit alike with either race.
His arms were all his own, our Europe's growth,
Which two worlds bless for civilising both;
The musket swung behind his shoulders broad,
And somewhat stooped by his marine abode,
But brawny as the boar's; and hung beneath,
His cutlass drooped, unconscious of a sheath,
Or lost or worn away; his pistols were
Linked to his belt, a matrimonial pair—
(Let not this metaphor appear a scoff,
Though one missed fire, the other would go off);
These, with a bayonet, not so free from rust
As when the arm-chest held its brighter trust,
Completed his accoutrements, as Night
Surveyed him in his garb heteroclite.
"What cheer, Ben Bunting?" cried (when in full view
Our new acquaintance) Torquil. "Aught of new?"

"Ey, ey!" quoth Ben, "not new, but news enow;

A strange sail in the offing."—"Sail! and how?

What! could you make her out? It cannot be;

I've seen no rag of canvass on the sea."

"Belike," said Ben, "you might not from the bay,

But from the bluff-head, where I watched to-day,

I saw her in the doldrums; for the wind

Was light and baffling."—"When the Sun declined

Where lay she? had she anchored?"—"No, but still

She bore down on us, till the wind grew still."

"Her flag?"—"I had no glass: but fore and aft,

Egad! she seemed a wicked-looking craft."

"Armed?"—"I expect so;—sent on the look-out:

'Tis time, belike, to put our helm about."

"About?—Whate'er may have us now in chase,

We'll make no running fight, for that were base;

We will die at our quarters, like true men."

"Ey, ey! for that 'tis all the same to Ben."

"Does Christian know this?"—"Aye; he has piped all hands

To quarters. They are furbishing the stands

Of arms; and we have got some guns to bear,

And scaled them. You are wanted."—"That's but fair;

And if it were not, mine is not the soul

To leave my comrades helpless on the shoal.

My Neuha! ah! and must my fate pursue

Not me alone, but one so sweet and true?

But whatsoe'er betide, ah, Neuha! now

Unman me not: the hour will not allow

A tear; I am thine whatever intervenes!"

"Right," quoth Ben; "that will do for the marines.

CANTO THE THIRD

The fight was o'er; the flashing through the gloom,
Which robes the cannon as he wings a tomb,
Had ceased; and sulphury vapours upward driven
Had left the Earth, and but polluted Heaven:
The rattling roar which rung in every volley
Had left the echoes to their melancholy;
No more they shrieked their horror, boom for boom;
The strife was done, the vanquished had their doom;
The mutineers were crushed, dispersed, or ta'en,
Or lived to deem the happiest were the slain.
Few, few escaped, and these were hunted o'er
The isle they loved beyond their native shore.
No further home was theirs, it seemed, on earth,
Once renegades to that which gave them birth;
Tracked like wild beasts, like them they sought the wild,
As to a Mother's bosom flies the child;
But vainly wolves and lions seek their den,
And still more vainly men escape from men.

Beneath a rock whose jutting base protrudes

Far over Ocean in its fiercest moods,

When scaling his enormous crag the wave

Is hurled down headlong, like the foremost brave,

And falls back on the foaming crowd behind,

Which fight beneath the banners of the wind,

But now at rest, a little remnant drew

Together, bleeding, thirsty, faint, and few;

But still their weapons in their hands, and still

With something of the pride of former will,

As men not all unused to meditate,

And strive much more than wonder at their fate.

Their present lot was what they had foreseen,

And dared as what was likely to have been;

Yet still the lingering hope, which deemed their lot

Not pardoned, but unsought for or forgot,

Or trusted that, if sought, their distant caves

Might still be missed amidst the world of waves,

Had weaned their thoughts in part from what they saw

And felt, the vengeance of their country's law.

Their sea-green isle, their guilt-won Paradise,
No more could shield their Virtue or their Vice:
Their better feelings, if such were, were thrown
Back on themselves,—their sins remained alone.
Proscribed even in their second country, they
Were lost; in vain the World before them lay;
All outlets seemed secured. Their new allies
Had fought and bled in mutual sacrifice;
But what availed the club and spear, and arm
Of Hercules, against the sulphury charm,
The magic of the thunder, which destroyed
The warrior ere his strength could be employed?
Dug, like a spreading pestilence, the grave
No less of human bravery than the brave!
Their own scant numbers acted all the few
Against the many oft will dare and do;
But though the choice seems native to die free,
Even Greece can boast but one Thermopylæ,
Till now, when she has forged her broken chain
Back to a sword, and dies and lives again!

Beside the jutting rock the few appeared,

Like the last remnant of the red-deer's herd;

Their eyes were feverish, and their aspect worn,

But still the hunter's blood was on their horn.

A little stream came tumbling from the height,

And straggling into ocean as it might,

Its bounding crystal frolicked in the ray,

And gushed from cliff to crag with saltless spray;

Close on the wild, wide ocean, yet as pure

And fresh as Innocence, and more secure,

Its silver torrent glittered o'er the deep,

As the shy chamois' eye o'erlooks the steep,

While far below the vast and sullen swell

Of Ocean's alpine azure rose and fell.

To this young spring they rushed,—all feelings first

Absorbed in Passion's and in Nature's thirst,—

Drank as they do who drink their last, and threw

Their arms aside to revel in its dew;

Cooled their scorched throats, and washed the gory stains

From wounds whose only bandage might be chains;

Then, when their drought was quenched, looked sadly round,

As wondering how so many still were found

Alive and fetterless:—but silent all,

Each sought his fellow's eyes, as if to call

On him for language which his lips denied,

As though their voices with their cause had died.

Stern, and aloof a little from the rest,

Stood Christian, with his arms across his chest.

The ruddy, reckless, dauntless hue once spread

Along his cheek was livid now as lead;

His light-brown locks, so graceful in their flow,

Now rose like startled vipers o'er his brow.

Still as a statue, with his lips comprest

To stifle even the breath within his breast,

Fast by the rock, all menacing, but mute,

He stood; and, save a slight beat of his foot,

Which deepened now and then the sandy dint

Beneath his heel, his form seemed turned to flint.

Some paces further Torquil leaned his head

Against a bank, and spoke not, but he bled,—

Not mortally:—his worst wound was within;

His brow was pale, his blue eyes sunken in,

And blood-drops, sprinkled o'er his yellow hair,

Showed that his faintness came not from despair,

But Nature's ebb. Beside him was another,

Rough as a bear, but willing as a brother,—

Ben Bunting, who essayed to wash, and wipe,

And bind his wound—then calmly lit his pipe,

A trophy which survived a hundred fights,

A beacon which had cheered ten thousand nights.

The fourth and last of this deserted group

Walked up and down—at times would stand, then stoop

To pick a pebble up—then let it drop—

Then hurry as in haste—then quickly stop—

Then cast his eyes on his companions—then

Half whistle half a tune, and pause again—

And then his former movements would redouble,

With something between carelessness and trouble.

This is a long description, but applies

To scarce five minutes passed before the eyes;

But yet what minutes! Moments like to these

Rend men's lives into immortalities.

At length Jack Skyscrape, a mercurial man,

Who fluttered over all things like a fan,

More brave than firm, and more disposed to dare

And die at once than wrestle with despair,

Exclaimed, "G—d damn!"—those syllables intense,—

Nucleus of England's native eloquence,

As the Turk's "Allah!" or the Roman's more

Pagan "Proh Jupiter!" was wont of yore

To give their first impressions such a vent,

By way of echo to embarrassment.

Jack was embarrassed,—never hero more,

And as he knew not what to say, he swore:

Nor swore in vain; the long congenial sound

Revived Ben Bunting from his pipe profound;

He drew it from his mouth, and looked full wise,

But merely added to the oath his eyes;

Thus rendering the imperfect phrase complete,

A peroration I need not repeat.

But Christian, of a higher order, stood

Like an extinct volcano in his mood;

Silent, and sad, and savage,—with the trace

Of passion reeking from his clouded face;

Till lifting up again his sombre eye,

It glanced on Torquil, who leaned faintly by.

"And is it thus?" he cried, "unhappy boy!

And thee, too, thee—my madness must destroy!"

He said, and strode to where young Torquil stood,

Yet dabbled with his lately flowing blood;

Seized his hand wistfully, but did not press,

And shrunk as fearful of his own caress;

Enquired into his state: and when he heard

The wound was slighter than he deemed or feared,

A moment's brightness passed along his brow,

As much as such a moment would allow.

"Yes," he exclaimed, "we are taken in the toil,

But not a coward or a common spoil;

Dearly they have bought us—dearly still may buy,—

And I must fall; but have you strength to fly?

'Twould be some comfort still, could you survive;

Our dwindled band is now too few to strive.

Oh! for a sole canoe! though but a shell,

To bear you hence to where a hope may dwell!

For me, my lot is what I sought; to be,

In life or death, the fearless and the free."

Even as he spoke, around the promontory,

Which nodded o'er the billows high and hoary,

A dark speck dotted Ocean: on it flew

Like to the shadow of a roused sea-mew;

Onward it came—and, lo! a second followed—

Now seen—now hid—where Ocean's vale was hollowed;

And near, and nearer, till the dusky crew

Presented well-known aspects to the view,

Till on the surf their skimming paddles play,

Buoyant as wings, and flitting through the spray;—

Now perching on the wave's high curl, and now

Dashed downward in the thundering foam below,

Which flings it broad and boiling sheet on sheet,

And slings its high flakes, shivered into sleet:

But floating still through surf and swell, drew nigh
The barks, like small birds through a lowering sky.
Their art seemed nature—such the skill to sweep
The wave of these born playmates of the deep.
And who the first that, springing on the strand,
Leaped like a Nereid from her shell to land,
With dark but brilliant skin, and dewy eye
Shining with love, and hope, and constancy?
Neuha—the fond, the faithful, the adored—
Her heart on Torquil's like a torrent poured;
And smiled, and wept, and near, and nearer clasped,
As if to be assured 'twas him she grasped;
Shuddered to see his yet warm wound, and then,
To find it trivial, smiled and wept again.
She was a warrior's daughter, and could bear
Such sights, and feel, and mourn, but not despair.
Her lover lived,—nor foes nor fears could blight
That full-blown moment in its all delight:
Joy trickled in her tears, joy filled the sob
That rocked her heart till almost HEARD to throb;

And Paradise was breathing in the sigh

Of Nature's child in Nature's ecstasy.

The sterner spirits who beheld that meeting

Were not unmoved; who are, when hearts are greeting?

Even Christian gazed upon the maid and boy

With tearless eye, but yet a gloomy joy

Mixed with those bitter thoughts the soul arrays

In hopeless visions of our better days,

When all's gone—to the rainbow's latest ray.

"And but for me!" he said, and turned away;

Then gazed upon the pair, as in his den

A lion looks upon his cubs again;

And then relapsed into his sullen guise,

As heedless of his further destinies.

But brief their time for good or evil thought;

The billows round the promontory brought

The plash of hostile oars.—Alas! who made

That sound a dread? All around them seemed arrayed

Against them, save the bride of Toobonai:

She, as she caught the first glimpse o'er the bay

Of the armed boats, which hurried to complete
The remnant's ruin with their flying feet,
Beckoned the natives round her to their prows,
Embarked their guests and launched their light canoes;
In one placed Christian and his comrades twain—
But she and Torquil must not part again.
She fixed him in her own.—Away! away!
They cleared the breakers, dart along the bay,
And towards a group of islets, such as bear
The sea-bird's nest and seal's surf-hollowed lair,
They skim the blue tops of the billows; fast
They flew, and fast their fierce pursuers chased.
They gain upon them—now they lose again,—
Again make way and menace o'er the main;
And now the two canoes in chase divide,
And follow different courses o'er the tide,
To baffle the pursuit.—Away! away!
As Life is on each paddle's flight to-day,
And more than Life or lives to Neuha: Love
Freights the frail bark and urges to the cove;
And now the refuge and the foe are nigh—
Yet, yet a moment! Fly, thou light ark, fly!

CANTO THE FOURTH

White as a white sail on a dusky sea,

When half the horizon's clouded and half free,

Fluttering between the dun wave and the sky,

Is Hope's last gleam in Man's extremity.

Her anchor parts; but still her snowy sail

Attracts our eye amidst the rudest gale:

Though every wave she climbs divides us more,

The heart still follows from the loneliest shore.

Not distant from the isle of Toobonai,

A black rock rears its bosom o'er the spray,

The haunt of birds, a desert to mankind,

Where the rough seal reposes from the wind,

And sleeps unwieldy in his cavern dun,

Or gambols with huge frolic in the sun:

There shrilly to the passing oar is heard

The startled echo of the Ocean bird,

Who rears on its bare breast her callow brood,

The feathered fishers of the solitude.

A narrow segment of the yellow sand

On one side forms the outline of a strand;

Here the young turtle, crawling from his shell,

Steals to the deep wherein his parents dwell;

Chipped by the beam, a nursling of the day,

But hatched for ocean by the fostering ray;

The rest was one bleak precipice, as e'er

Gave mariners a shelter and despair;

A spot to make the saved regret the deck

Which late went down, and envy the lost wreck.

Such was the stern asylum Neuha chose

To shield her lover from his following foes;

But all its secret was not told; she knew

In this a treasure hidden from the view.

Ere the canoes divided, near the spot,

The men that manned what held her Torquil's lot,

By her command removed, to strengthen more

The skiff which wafted Christian from the shore.

This he would have opposed; but with a smile

She pointed calmly to the craggy isle,

And bade him "speed and prosper." She would take

The rest upon herself for Torquil's sake.

They parted with this added aid; afar,

The Proa darted like a shooting star,

And gained on the pursuers, who now steered

Right on the rock which she and Torquil neared.

They pulled; her arm, though delicate, was free

And firm as ever grappled with the sea,

And yielded scarce to Torquil's manlier strength.

The prow now almost lay within its length

Of the crag's steep inexorable face,

With nought but soundless waters for its base;

Within a hundred boats' length was the foe,

And now what refuge but their frail canoe?

This Torquil asked with half upbraiding eye,

Which said—"Has Neuha brought me here to die?

Is this a place of safety, or a grave,

And yon huge rock the tombstone of the wave?"

They rested on their paddles, and uprose

Neuha, and pointing to the approaching foes,

Cried, "Torquil, follow me, and fearless follow!"

Then plunged at once into the Ocean's hollow.

There was no time to pause—the foes were near—
Chains in his eye, and menace in his ear;
With vigour they pulled on, and as they came,
Hailed him to yield, and by his forfeit name.
Headlong he leapt—to him the swimmer's skill
Was native, and now all his hope from ill:
But how, or where? He dived, and rose no more;
The boat's crew looked amazed o'er sea and shore.
There was no landing on that precipice,
Steep, harsh, and slippery as a berg of ice.
They watched awhile to see him float again,
But not a trace rebubbled from the main:
The wave rolled on, no ripple on its face,
Since their first plunge recalled a single trace;
The little whirl which eddied, and slight foam,
That whitened o'er what seemed their latest home,
White as a sepulchre above the pair
Who left no marble (mournful as an heir)
The quiet Proa wavering o'er the tide
Was all that told of Torquil and his bride;

And but for this alone the whole might seem

The vanished phantom of a seaman's dream.

They paused and searched in vain, then pulled away;

Even Superstition now forbade their stay.

Some said he had not plunged into the wave,

But vanished like a corpse-light from a grave;

Others, that something supernatural

Glared in his figure, more than mortal tall;

While all agreed that in his cheek and eye

There was a dead hue of Eternity.

Still as their oars receded from the crag,

Round every weed a moment would they lag,

Expectant of some token of their prey;

But no—he had melted from them like the spray.

And where was he the Pilgrim of the Deep,

Following the Nereid? Had they ceased to weep

For ever? or, received in coral caves,

Wrung life and pity from the softening waves?

Did they with Ocean's hidden sovereigns dwell,

And sound with Mermen the fantastic shell?

Did Neuha with the mermaids comb her hair
Flowing o'er ocean as it streamed in air?
Or had they perished, and in silence slept
Beneath the gulf wherein they boldly leapt?
Young Neuha plunged into the deep, and he
Followed: her track beneath her native sea
Was as a native's of the element,
So smoothly—bravely—brilliantly she went,
Leaving a streak of light behind her heel,
Which struck and flashed like an amphibious steel,
Closely, and scarcely less expert to trace
The depths where divers hold the pearl in chase,
Torquil, the nursling of the northern seas,
Pursued her liquid steps with heart and ease.
Deep—deeper for an instant Neuha led
The way—then upward soared—and as she spread
Her arms, and flung the foam from off her locks,
Laughed, and the sound was answered by the rocks.
They had gained a central realm of earth again,
But looked for tree, and field, and sky, in vain.

Around she pointed to a spacious cave,

Whose only portal was the keyless wave,

(A hollow archway by the sun unseen,

Save through the billows' glassy veil of green,

In some transparent ocean holiday,

When all the finny people are at play,)

Wiped with her hair the brine from Torquil's eyes,

And clapped her hands with joy at his surprise;

Led him to where the rock appeared to jut,

And form a something like a Triton's hut;

For all was darkness for a space, till day,

Through clefts above let in a sobered ray;

As in some old cathedral's glimmering aisle

The dusty monuments from light recoil,

Thus sadly in their refuge submarine

The vault drew half her shadow from the scene.

Forth from her bosom the young savage drew

A pine torch, strongly girded with gnatoo;

A plantain-leaf o'er all, the more to keep

Its latent sparkle from the sapping deep.

This mantle kept it dry; then from a nook
Of the same plantain-leaf a flint she took,
A few shrunk withered twigs, and from the blade
Of Torquil's knife struck fire, and thus arrayed
The grot with torchlight. Wide it was and high,
And showed a self-born Gothic canopy;
The arch upreared by Nature's architect,
The architrave some Earthquake might erect;
The buttress from some mountain's bosom hurled,
When the Poles crashed, and water was the world;
Or hardened from some earth-absorbing fire,
While yet the globe reeked from its funeral pyre;
The fretted pinnacle, the aisle, the nave,
Were there, all scooped by Darkness from her cave.
There, with a little tinge of phantasy,
Fantastic faces moped and mowed on high,
And then a mitre or a shrine would fix
The eye upon its seeming crucifix.
Thus Nature played with the stalactites,
And built herself a Chapel of the Seas.

And Neuha took her Torquil by the hand,
And waved along the vault her kindled brand,
And led him into each recess, and showed
The secret places of their new abode.
Nor these alone, for all had been prepared
Before, to soothe the lover's lot she shared:
The mat for rest; for dress the fresh gnatoo,
And sandal oil to fence against the dew;
For food the cocoa-nut, the yam, the bread
Born of the fruit; for board the plantain spread
With its broad leaf, or turtle-shell which bore
A banquet in the flesh it covered o'er;
The gourd with water recent from the rill,
The ripe banana from the mellow hill;
A pine-torch pile to keep undying light,
And she herself, as beautiful as night,
To fling her shadowy spirit o'er the scene,
And make their subterranean world serene.
She had foreseen, since first the stranger's sail
Drew to their isle, that force or flight might fail,

And formed a refuge of the rocky den

For Torquil's safety from his countrymen.

Each dawn had wafted there her light canoe,

Laden with all the golden fruits that grew;

Each eve had seen her gliding through the hour

With all could cheer or deck their sparry bower;

And now she spread her little store with smiles,

The happiest daughter of the loving isles.

She, as he gazed with grateful wonder, pressed

Her sheltered love to her impassioned breast;

And suited to her soft caresses, told

An olden tale of Love,—for Love is old,

Old as eternity, but not outworn

With each new being born or to be born:

How a young Chief, a thousand moons ago,

Diving for turtle in the depths below,

Had risen, in tracking fast his ocean prey,

Into the cave which round and o'er them lay;

How, in some desperate feud of after-time,

He sheltered there a daughter of the clime,

A foe beloved, and offspring of a foe,
Saved by his tribe but for a captive's woe;
How, when the storm of war was stilled, he led
His island clan to where the waters spread
Their deep-green shadow o'er the rocky door,
Then dived—it seemed as if to rise no more:
His wondering mates, amazed within their bark,
Or deemed him mad, or prey to the blue shark;
Rowed round in sorrow the sea-girded rock,
Then paused upon their paddles from the shock;
When, fresh and springing from the deep, they saw
A Goddess rise—so deemed they in their awe;
And their companion, glorious by her side,
Proud and exulting in his Mermaid bride;
And how, when undeceived, the pair they bore
With sounding conchs and joyous shouts to shore;
How they had gladly lived and calmly died,—
And why not also Torquil and his bride?
Not mine to tell the rapturous caress
Which followed wildly in that wild recess

This tale; enough that all within that cave
Was love, though buried strong as in the grave,
Where Abelard, through twenty years of death,
When Eloïsa's form was lowered beneath
Their nuptial vault, his arms outstretched, and pressed
The kindling ashes to his kindled breast.
The waves without sang round their couch, their roar
As much unheeded as if life were o'er;
Within, their hearts made all their harmony,
Love's broken murmur and more broken sigh.
And they, the cause and sharers of the shock
Which left them exiles of the hollow rock,
Where were they? O'er the sea for life they plied,
To seek from Heaven the shelter men denied.
Another course had been their choice—but where?
The wave which bore them still their foes would bear,
Who, disappointed of their former chase,
In search of Christian now renewed their race.
Eager with anger, their strong arms made way,
Like vultures baffled of their previous prey.

They gained upon them, all whose safety lay
In some bleak crag or deeply-hidden bay:
No further chance or choice remained; and right
For the first further rock which met their sight
They steered, to take their latest view of land,
And yield as victims, or die sword in hand;
Dismissed the natives and their shallop, who
Would still have battled for that scanty crew;
But Christian bade them seek their shore again,
Nor add a sacrifice which were in vain;
For what were simple bow and savage spear
Against the arms which must be wielded here?
They landed on a wild but narrow scene,
Where few but Nature's footsteps yet had been;
Prepared their arms, and with that gloomy eye,
Stern and sustained, of man's extremity,
When Hope is gone, nor Glory's self remains
To cheer resistance against death or chains.—
They stood, the three, as the three hundred stood
Who dyed Thermopylæ with holy blood.

But, ah! how different! 'tis the cause makes all,

Degrades or hallows courage in its fall.

O'er them no fame, eternal and intense,

Blazed through the clouds of Death and beckoned
hence;

No grateful country, smiling through her tears,

Begun the praises of a thousand years;

No nation's eyes would on their tomb be bent,

No heroes envy them their monument;

However boldly their warm blood was spilt,

Their Life was shame, their Epitaph was guilt.

And this they knew and felt, at least the one,

The leader of the band he had undone;

Who, born perchance for better things, had set

His life upon a cast which lingered yet:

But now the die was to be thrown, and all

The chances were in favour of his fall:

And such a fall! But still he faced the shock,

Obdurate as a portion of the rock

Whereon he stood, and fixed his levelled gun,

Dark as a sullen cloud before the sun.

The boat drew nigh, well armed, and firm the crew

To act whatever Duty bade them do;

Careless of danger, as the onward wind

Is of the leaves it strews, nor looks behind.

And, yet, perhaps, they rather wished to go

Against a nation's than a native foe,

And felt that this poor victim of self-will,

Briton no more, had once been Britain's still.

They hailed him to surrender—no reply;

Their arms were poised, and glittered in the sky.

They hailed again—no answer; yet once more

They offered quarter louder than before.

The echoes only, from the rock's rebound,

Took their last farewell of the dying sound.

Then flashed the flint, and blazed the volleying flame,

And the smoke rose between them and their aim,

While the rock rattled with the bullets' knell,

Which pealed in vain, and flattened as they fell;

Then flew the only answer to be given

By those who had lost all hope in earth or heaven.

After the first fierce peal as they pulled nigher,

They heard the voice of Christian shout, "Now, fire!"

And ere the word upon the echo died,

Two fell; the rest assailed the rock's rough side,

And, furious at the madness of their foes,

Disdained all further efforts, save to close.

But steep the crag, and all without a path,

Each step opposed a bastion to their wrath,

While, placed 'midst clefts the least accessible,

Which Christian's eye was trained to mark full well,

The three maintained a strife which must not yield,

In spots where eagles might have chosen to build.

Their every shot told; while the assailant fell,

Dashed on the shingles like the limpet shell;

But still enough survived, and mounted still,

Scattering their numbers here and there, until

Surrounded and commanded, though not nigh

Enough for seizure, near enough to die,

The desperate trio held aloof their fate

But by a thread, like sharks who have gorged the bait;

Yet to the very last they battled well,

And not a groan informed their foes who fell.

Christian died last—twice wounded; and once more

Mercy was offered when they saw his gore;

Too late for life, but not too late to die,

With, though a hostile hand, to close his eye.

A limb was broken, and he drooped along

The crag, as doth a falcon reft of young.

The sound revived him, or appeared to wake

Some passion which a weakly gesture spake:

He beckoned to the foremost, who drew nigh,

But, as they neared, he reared his weapon high—

His last ball had been aimed, but from his breast

He tore the topmost button from his vest,

Down the tube dashed it—levelled—fired, and smiled

As his foe fell; then, like a serpent, coiled

His wounded, weary form, to where the steep

Looked desperate as himself along the deep;

Cast one glance back, and clenched his hand, and shook

His last rage 'gainst the earth which he forsook;

Then plunged: the rock below received like glass

His body crushed into one gory mass,

With scarce a shred to tell of human form,

Or fragment for the sea-bird or the worm;

A fair-haired scalp, besmeared with blood and weeds,

Yet reeked, the remnant of himself and deeds;

Some splinters of his weapons (to the last,

As long as hand could hold, he held them fast)

Yet glittered, but at distance—hurled away

To rust beneath the dew and dashing spray.

The rest was nothing—save a life mis-spent,

And soul—but who shall answer where it went?

'Tis ours to bear, not judge the dead; and they

Who doom to Hell, themselves are on the way,

Unless these bullies of eternal pains

Are pardoned their bad hearts for their worse brains.

The deed was over! All were gone or ta'en,

The fugitive, the captive, or the slain.

Chained on the deck, where once, a gallant crew,

They stood with honour, were the wretched few

Survivors of the skirmish on the isle;

But the last rock left no surviving spoil.

Cold lay they where they fell, and weltering,

While o'er them flapped the sea-birds' dewy wing,

Now wheeling nearer from the neighbouring surge,

And screaming high their harsh and hungry dirge:

But calm and careless heaved the wave below,

Eternal with unsympathetic flow;

Far o'er its face the Dolphins sported on,

And sprung the flying fish against the sun,

Till its dried wing relapsed from its brief height,

To gather moisture for another flight.

'Twas morn; and Neuha, who by dawn of day

Swam smoothly forth to catch the rising ray,

And watch if aught approached the amphibious lair

Where lay her lover, saw a sail in air:

It flapped, it filled, and to the growing gale

Bent its broad arch: her breath began to fail

With fluttering fear, her heart beat thick and high,

While yet a doubt sprung where its course might lie.

But no! it came not; fast and far away
The shadow lessened as it cleared the bay.
She gazed, and flung the sea-foam from her eyes,
To watch as for a rainbow in the skies.
On the horizon verged the distant deck,
Diminished, dwindled to a very speck—
Then vanished. All was Ocean, all was Joy!
Down plunged she through the cave to rouse her boy;
Told all she had seen, and all she hoped, and all
That happy love could augur or recall;
Sprung forth again, with Torquil following free
His bounding Nereid over the broad sea;
Swam round the rock, to where a shallow cleft
Hid the canoe that Neuha there had left
Drifting along the tide, without an oar,
That eve the strangers chased them from the shore;
But when these vanished, she pursued her prow,
Regained, and urged to where they found it now:
Nor ever did more love and joy embark,
Than now were wafted in that slender ark.

Again their own shore rises on the view,

No more polluted with a hostile hue;

No sullen ship lay bristling o'er the foam,

A floating dungeon:—all was Hope and Home!

A thousand Proas darted o'er the bay,

With sounding shells, and heralded their way;

The chiefs came down, around the people poured,

And welcomed Torquil as a son restored;

The women thronged, embracing and embraced

By Neuha, asking where they had been chased,

And how escaped? The tale was told; and then

One acclamation rent the sky again;

And from that hour a new tradition gave

Their sanctuary the name of "Neuha's Cave."

A hundred fires, far flickering from the height,

Blazed o'er the general revel of the night,

The feast in honour of the guest, returned

To Peace and Pleasure, perilously earned;

A night succeeded by such happy days

As only the yet infant world displays.

END

OGRE

Crouched beneath the branches, in the shade,

An ogre peeled its eyes. Its skin of green

did mask its hulking presence from the greyed

and wilted man, from whom it stayed unseen.

The ogre watched in wait and made no sound.

The man had naught for armour, but was gowned

in tough yet tattered cloth against the cold.

He journeyed from the tavern, where he'd drowned

an early morning fear of growing old –

And now, he stumbled forth – his world in spin.

A hammer at an anvil joined the din

of village streets alive with market trade.

The man, whose purse on better days was thin,

Avoided scents of food, to not be swayed,

As, he would need his coin for evening's mead.

At least that's what he thought, as, arrow freed –

From crude, unpolished wood that shaped a bow –

would coax a spattered flower bloom from seed,

Swift planted 'fore the man could ever know

His final moment living joined the Past.

Nearby, the cobbler's son did freeze, aghast.
He'd witnessed as the drunkard struck the dirt.

The ogre nocked a second arrow fast,

And levelled it towards the boy's new shirt –

A shirt the cobbler's wife was yet to see.

With aim to raise the body count to three,

The ogre drew a blade and found a mark,

And clambered from the branches of the tree,

and slashed until the target's eyes were dark.

Then, all at once, the end to killing came.

A woman stood, whose face was not the same

as anyone who in the past had seen

those other times, come sun or snow or rain

when ogre'd tried to pick the village clean,

And only ceased when guards made for his head.

But not today. This woman, now, instead

Did raise her arms, her lip began to shake.

"What is the reason that you leave us dead,

With no regard for chaos in your wake?"

She asked as widened eyes began to well.

To her surprise, the ogre tried to tell

of why he acted so without regard.

His words were jumbled, and their purpose fell,

As he, confused, did find it rather hard

to form a meaning with the spoken word.

The ogre found his mumbling quite absurd –

To think, he'd stand in village square and speak!

And yet, now that he spoke, he felt deterred

from killing, but to save appearing weak,

He tensed his arms and growled a mighty growl.

The woman met his anger with a scowl,

While many other villagers stepped back.

"You'd have us think of you as fierce and foul,"

She said, "but all I see is what you lack."

The ogre, quite ashamed, then walked away.

He sat beneath a tree and watched the day,
As, peacefully, it shared its place with night.
And there, for all the stars, he'd finally say
aloud the many things that caused his plight,
When, unexpectedly, the stars replied.

The ogre thought this moment he had died,
And now engaged the chorus of the Gods.
He shrank and gripped his head, but could not hide –
With sanity, he found himself at odds –
Yet still, with covered ears, he heard the voice.

"To us, it seems, you struggle with a choice."
The stars did say, and shimmered from above.
"To take a life, or with one to rejoice?
You make them flee and never share their love,
and now you wonder at another way."

The ogre, stunned, knew not what he should say,

And found no words for thoughts inside his head.

Before day's noon, the only card he'd play

was breach the walls and leave as many dead

as fear and frequent slashing would allow.

And yet, now sat perplexed against the bough,

The stars, which till tonight did stay unseen,

Grew brighter still, and asked of him to vow

to shelve his bow and keep his dagger clean.

"I can't," the ogre grizzled through his teeth.

"I've not a shelf, a locker nor a sheath,"

He whined and shrugged and turned his face from sky.

"I've nothing of such likeness to bequeath."

And once again ashamed, with downcast eye,

He felt the forceful gaze of cosmic judge.

"The choice is yours. Beware, do not begrudge
the pledges that you make this very night.
Be earnest. Strive through all the pain to drudge,
And surely you will see the dawn's new light.
Though heed these words, this path shall not return."

The ogre shook his head, "But did I earn
the right to make amends - to start anew?
Much easier to let the buildings burn,
Then change my very being, through and through."
The stars exhaled a sigh that cooled the air.

"If easy is your goal, then you are there.
To blame your being – easy it must be,
While still you kill and maim without a care.
Though not until you *choose*, will you be free.
To act without a thought makes you a beast."

"I choose to make of humans then a feast!"

The ogre, insincerely, taunted sky.

"Then do it." Said the stars, "Let soon deceased

be no such match for fury you'll let fly.

Give all your strength, and know it be your whim."

"You mock me." Ogre's voice was rough and grim,

Though grew less so with every hour passed.

"There's no such option, life for me is dim -

Forever I am moulded by my caste.

You know this to be true – still, you critique."

"The only truth I know, is just how bleak

the future and your life, to you, does seem.

But contemplate on what you'll never seek

without considered thought - without a dream.

You'll hunt until you're caught. And that is all."

"Direct me!" Ogre sobbed, "before I fall

a victim of my own destructive way!

And with your help I'll learn again to crawl."

The stars gleamed brighter, "be that as it may,

Change cannot come from far above the sky."

"Then what am I to do?" The ogre's cry

did echo 'cross the dark and empty field.

He raged and huffed and growled with no reply.

"You bring no help! Like blades, these words you wield!"

The stars, still silent, dimmed against the deep.

The ogre, scared, alone, began to weep.

Abandoned as he was, beneath the tree.

His racing mind did all to fight off sleep,

But finally, at dawn, it set him free,

And, restless, there he slept, till coming noon.

A songbird woke him with a whistling tune,

And Ogre snarled and swatted at the air.

Forgiven he would be to not attune

So quickly to the words of star affair –

Though at his actions, panic gripped his chest.

"Apologies," growled Ogre to the nest,

In which the songbird sat and glanced below -

"That habit needs to die with all the rest.

Regard it not, your song I'd like to know."

And patiently the ogre tuned his ear.

And sing he did, that songbird, whistling clear

great many tunes of generations past.

At first, the ogre struggling to hear

the nuances now flowing loud and fast -

Yet with the passing day, his knowledge grew.

"Such wisdom in such small a beast - who knew?"
The ogre, frightful grinning, did exclaim.
He raised a hand, to which the songbird flew.
"Why ever would one choose of you to maim?"
The silent stars aglow with their delight.

A million specks joined canvas of the night,
And, curious, they stayed to peer below.
A distant call urged singing bird to flight –
Together playing in adagio –
And sorrow stayed, for Ogre there to quell.

Of life without more songs, he could not dwell
And, leaving by the tree his bow and blade,
The ogre raced towards the village bell
and bustling carts and tools of metal made,
For empty did his world so quickly seem.

He recognised the molten iron's scream

Yet never had he marvelled at the skill –

He watched a turning wheel sat in a stream,

Though knew not of the farmer or the mill.

And never had it crossed his mind to ask.

He felt he'd worn, for all his life, a mask,

Unnoticed, while it served a filtered view.

He'd only ever drank to drain the cask,

Without a care from whence did come the brew.

Yet sudden, all at once, he asked these things;

He spied the turrets – what are Queens and Kings?

And how are they so different from the rest?

He pondered guards with clothes of metal rings -

Why should they act as others do behest?

He then considered life within his clan.

The ogres seemed the same, yet unlike man,

Their craftsmanship did end with bone for blade.

No anvils in their cave, no grain-wheel ran,

And certainly, no garments could be made.

Indeed, his very shawl was from the town!

In questions, now, his mind did slowly drown,

As chimney smoke rose high on distant hill –

With opened eyes, his world turned upside-down.

His heart and lungs now fluttered at the thrill.

A childish curiosity took hold.

With forceful winds he spurred his pace twofold

towards the houses, where before he'd slain.

Armed not, except with questions, he would hold

a forum, where the humans could explain –

And then he'd ask forgiveness for his ways.

He saw himself, in dialogue, for days,
With intrigue, as each villager stepped up.
They'd plea that he participate in plays,
And then invite their newfound friend to sup –
A growing love brought tears to Ogre's eye.

He pictured how he'd teach them best to pry
the cage of ribs from pig, or goat, or sheep.
Return would people show the ogre why
they churned the earth and threw nets to the deep –
Together they'd expand on all they knew.

He clambered over walls and bushes – through,
Until the bustling Inn was at his side.
"Good people!" greeted Ogre, smiling too –
Those sharp, foreboding teeth he could not hide –
"I stand before you, not as fiend or foe."

The people screamed, for, they could never know

how different and sincere the ogre felt.

The women grabbed at stones and aimed to throw,

As drunken men drew weapons from their belt.

The ogre, in confusion, raised his hand.

"Oh villagers, you do not understand–"

A whistling stone did clack against his jaw.

"That hurts!" He yelped. "This is not what I'd
                              planned."

But in a boiling rage the crowd flung more.

Amidst the hail of stones, the ogre wept.

Each stone a small repayment for his debt.

Ignoring sobs, the village did not cease.

While crumpling to the ground, the ogre kept

his face towards the sky and begged for peace,

And watched as stars did slowly disappear.

The villagers made their intentions clear –

Enough of always looking to their back,

Afraid a hateful ogre, stalking near

was poised to launch a deadly, swift attack –

So now they'd claim a body of their own.

'Ogre'

Jonathon Best 2021

More poetry and pocket classics at jbestbooks.com

ISBN: 978-0-9953520-2-5

www.ingramcontent.com/pod-product-compliance
Lightning Source LLC
Chambersburg PA
CBHW030454010526
44118CB00011B/940